D1366465

ME AND MY FEELINGS

JILLIAN POWELL

SEA-TO-SEA

Mankato Collingwood London

Problem Page
Me and my feelings

Working out our feelings is not always easy, especially when we are growing up. The letters, emails, and texts in this book are all from young people who are worried about something. Some have chosen to confide in friends, while others have written to an advice column. A few have only told their diaries...

Dear reader

The postal addresses used in this book have all been changed to fictitious places. The email addresses have also been censored. All the photographs are posed by models.

I hate being so shy

Dear Sam

I find it really hard to make new friends because I have always been really shy. I dry up when I try to talk to someone new—especially a girl. My hands go clammy and my heart races. Then I end up feeling really mad at myself.

Parties are a nightmare, because I can't think of anything to say. I just feel stupid. I am too scared to talk to anyone, and when I do try to join in on a group, everyone ignores me. I usually leave early, because I get tired of hanging around feeling like an idiot. How can I stop being so shy?

Ben, aged 14

327 Ridge Road
Adamsville

September 17

Dear Ben

Shyness is more common than you think—even top celebrities confess to it. It can be caused by a fear of being rejected, or having low self-esteem. It helps to take up new interests and hobbies. Even by going to see a new movie, or reading a book that's just out, you will have something to talk about.

If you feel nervous at a party, take some slow, deep breaths. Focus on other people around you: make eye contact, ask lots of questions, listen to people, and remember what they say. You'll find people will enjoy talking to you if you are interested in what they are saying.

Good luck!

Sam, Agony Uncle

Top Tips

Overcoming shyness

★ Take up a new sport or hobby or listen to a new CD—anything you can share with others.

★ At a party, set yourself a challenge of finding out three things about three new people: forget yourself and concentrate on others.

★ Smile! Smiles are great icebreakers.

★ Practice talking to one new person a week—even if it's just talking about the weather to someone on line at the corner store!

How does it feel to be shy?

I'm always a bit nervous about meeting new people. I don't think I have enough to say.

Shala, aged 13

I started at a new school and thought I'd never make friends because I'm so shy. It was okay though.

Paul, aged 11

I'm really jealous of my brother Richard. He's really chatty and I always get left out at parties and things.

Jamie, aged 10

Your Views

Have you ever felt shy? What's the best way you find to overcome shyness?

I don't think boys like me

From: EleanorB~~████████~~om
To: Mel6@~~████████~~m
Date: Tuesday, March 7
Subject: No one likes me!

Hi Mel,

Missing you like mad. Went to the ice-skating rink last night and it was the usual nightmare. There was this guy, Damian, who I really like. But he didn't even look my way. I felt like I was invisible, which was probably just as well because I had this huge zit on my cheek that made me look awful! I was wearing this new top and everything, and Shell had done my hair in a funky way, but I might as well have had a bag on my head! Maybe I should lose some weight. Mom says it's puppy fat, but sometimes I feel I look really fat. I don't think boys like me.

Hope you're okay, anyway. See you next week!

Ellie x

From: Mel6@~~████████~~
To: EleanorB@~~████████~~om
Date: Tuesday, March 7
Subject: Re: No one likes me!

Hi Ellie,

I wish you wouldn't do yourself down. You look great. You know I envy your hair! I bet it looked fantastic when Shell did it. You don't need to lose any weight either, you're great as you are. If this Damian can't see that, he's not worth having! We've been invited to a party when you come over next week. I'm sure you'll be a big hit!

See you then. Lots of love, Mel

The Facts

Self-esteem

❋ Body image is part of our self-esteem—how we think and feel about ourselves.

❋ Self-esteem is based on our inner feelings—not on facts.

❋ Some surveys show that only one percent of women are completely happy with their bodies.

❋ Problems like pimples and acne can lead to low self-esteem during puberty.

❋ Low self-esteem is linked to eating disorders including anorexia nervosa, bulimia, and binge eating.

Top Tips

Being happy about yourself

★ Accept there are some things you can't change about the way you look.

★ Concentrate on your best features—learn to make the most of them.

★ Try not to compare yourself with others—we are all individuals.

★ Every time you have a negative thought about yourself, counter it with a positive one—I may have acne, but I've got great eyes!

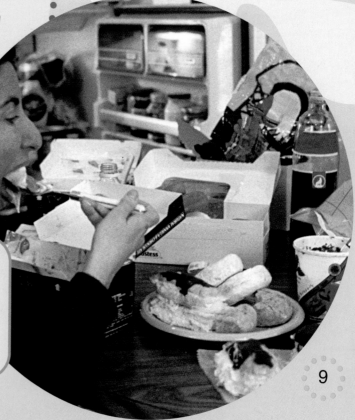

Your Views

What do you think Ellie can do to boost her self-esteem when she feels down?

I can't get over him

From: Jess231@v▓▓▓▓▓▓▓▓ess.com
To: agonyaunt@a▓▓▓▓▓▓ess.com
Date: Thursday, April 3
Subject: I can't get over my boyfriend

Dear Maggie,

A few months ago, my boyfriend and I split up. We had been going out for a few months and I thought we had something special. Then I found out he had been seeing someone else. I felt so stupid. It really hurt me and I was so angry with him. We had a huge argument and I split up with him. The trouble is, I really miss being with him. I keep wondering if we could still work things out. My best friend says I've got to move on, but how can I, when I still have these feelings for him?

Jessica, aged 14

From: agonyaunt@s▓▓▓▓▓▓dress.com
To: Jess231@▓▓▓▓▓▓om
Date: Monday, April 7
Subject: Re: I can't get over my boyfriend

Dear Jessica,

Getting over a relationship is tough, especially when you have been hurt. Before you can move on, you have to deal with your feelings. Every time you start thinking about your ex, stop yourself. Try saying, "I will think about that tomorrow!" If a positive thought about him comes into your head (he is so cool) counter it with a negative thought (he two-timed me).

Remember, you have feelings for the person you thought he was—not the person he is. Happier times are ahead. You just need to be ready for them.

Maggie, Agony Aunt

Top Tips

Getting over a breakup

⭐ Do things to boost your self-esteem—go out with friends, have some treats.

⭐ Make a list of all the things you didn't like about your ex.

⭐ Make a list of all the things you are looking for in a new relationship.

⭐ Get rid of anything that reminds you of your ex.

⭐ Delete his or her number from your phone book or cellphone so you can't phone them any more.

⭐ Avoid the people and places that remind you of your ex.

⭐ Tell yourself you will get over this, and you will feel better as time passes.

⭐ Get out to places where you have a chance to meet lots of new friends.

What do you think of relationships?

I think relationships at our age are taken far too seriously. When you're young, you should just chill out and enjoy yourself. I wouldn't even use the word "relationship." "Going out" is much less serious and more open.

Paul, aged 15

I've never had a serious relationship with a boy. I don't know what it feels like to be in love or have my heart broken.

Gemma, aged 13

My friend spent $50 on a boy to show her affection and the next day he dumped her. He never even gave the presents back.

Paula, aged 14

Your Views

How can Jessica get her ex out of her head?

My sister is hurting herself

325 Abigail Vale
Steelesville

November 28

Trish's advice column
Sorted magazine
Cedar Bluffs

Dear Trish

I am really worried about my sister Sophie. When I went into her room last night, I found her cutting her arms. She begged me not to tell anyone. She said it was the first time she had done it, but I saw a lot of marks and stuff on her arms. I think she must be really unhappy to do that but she made me swear not to tell so I don't know what to do. Could she really hurt herself? I keep thinking about it and I don't know whether I should tell anyone to make her stop.

Bridget, aged 14

Sophie's diary

29 November

Felt really ashamed last night because I started doing it again. My arm is a real mess. I had to wear long sleeves when I went out last night. Now Bridget has found out and if she tells Mom I am in trouble. I made her promise not to. Mom's got enough on her mind since Dad left.

325 Abigail Vale
Steelesville

Dear Bridget

Your sister is self-harming because she feels unhappy. Self-harm is a way of trying to blot out painful feelings, or to control at least one thing in her life. Although she has asked you not to tell, Sophie may need help to stop this. Cutting herself could cause lasting scars, or even lead to infection and health problems. If Sophie doesn't want to talk to your mom, she could see a youth counselor or doctor. Tell her you'll go with her. There are hotlines and organizations that can help too. If she refuses, you must tell your mom, or someone like a doctor, friend, or teacher.

Trish, Agony Aunt

The Facts

Self-harm

✳ Self-harm can include physical injuries such as cutting or burning the skin, pulling out hair, or taking dangerous drugs.

✳ It is a way of dealing with difficult feelings or emotions.

✳ It affects mainly teenage girls and young men in their early twenties.

✳ It is more common in children in one-parent families.

✳ Check out the websites on page 29 for more information and help.

Your Views

What can Bridget say to persuade her sister to get some help?

Exams are stressing me out

Hi Josh. U studying? Am panicking now!

Hi Nat. Yep. Doing Geog. Y r u panicking?

Shld have started sooner. Too much to do.

Nah, u r clever. U will sail thru! C u tomorrow.

Nat's diary

20 May

Dad is doing my head in, saying he expects me to do really well in the exams—I feel like I will be letting him down if I get low marks. I tried doing some math studying last night but my head was all over the place. I am so afraid I am going to let everyone down and mess things up.

Wish I'd started studying sooner.

Top Tips

Taking exams

★ Plan your study time—work out time slots for each subject.

★ Alternate favorite subjects with ones you like the least.

★ Try to make studying "active" rather than just rereading notes. Jot down pictures, diagrams, flashcards, mind maps—anything that will help ideas or images stay in your memory.

★ Don't be afraid to ask teachers for advice.

★ Take a short break every hour—it will keep your mind fresh.

★ Plan a few treats and use them as goals for when studying is done.

★ Keep things in perspective. Do your best and remember you can always retake some exams.

How do you cope with exams?

I can get so worked up I feel I am going to throw up before an exam.

Leila, aged 11

When you know that your parents and everyone are expecting you to get high marks, you can get really stressed worrying you are going to let everyone down.

Sanjay, aged 13

You can study so much that your brain gets stale and nothing goes in! You need to take breaks. I usually bounce a basketball around or go for a run. When I go back to it, I get a lot more done.

Mark, aged 13

Your Views

Do you think Nat is panicking for no reason? Do you think there is too much pressure applied when we take exams? How important are they?

I feel down all the time

V annoyed u r not coming out tonight Justin. 3rd time u have let us down! Paul

Justin u r really boring these days! Paul and I r really had it with u. Jez

Justin's diary

Friday, May 10

I was supposed to be going out with Paul and Jez tonight but I couldn't face it. I just feel so down all the time. Mom got mad at me again today because she can't get me up in the mornings, but I wake up feeling like I've got no energy to face the day. I feel so tired at school. We had music today but I don't even care about that any more. Now Paul and Jez are saying I'm boring, which makes me feel worse. I don't want to feel this way, but it's been going on a long time now—I'm not sure I will ever get out of this rut.

The Facts

Depression

✻ We all feel down at times, but if these feelings don't lift, we may have an illness called depression.

✻ About one in every 30 teenagers suffer from depression at some time.

✻ Someone who is depressed may need lots of sleep, or may sleep badly. They may lose their appetite, or "comfort eat." They often have no energy or interest in things, and feel low and tearful.

✻ Depression may run in families due to genetic factors.

✻ Depression seems to be linked with chemical changes in the part of the brain that controls mood. These changes prevent normal functioning of the brain and cause many of the symptoms of depression.

✻ It may help to see a doctor or a counselor because they can offer help and advice.

✻ Check out the websites on page 29 for more information and help.

Top Tips

Coping with depression

★ Make a pinboard or scrapbook and fill it with anything that is positive in your life. It could be a picture of a pet or a friend, or a reminder of something you have achieved.

★ Get physically active. It releases happy hormones called endorphins in the brain.

★ Don't bottle up feelings. It helps to talk over how you are feeling with others.

★ Make sure you do one thing every day that you enjoy.

★ Try to eat a healthy diet and eat and sleep at regular times.

Your Views

Should Paul and Jez have noticed the way Justin is feeling? What could they do to help him?

I can't stop this behavior

Sam's advice column
Sorted magazine
Cedar Bluffs

Dear Sam

Can you help? I think I'm going insane. The thing is I can't help doing things over and over again, like checking stuff inside my schoolbag, or shutting a door several times. I think it's getting worse. It makes me late for school because I have to check everything and do things so many times, and I sometimes miss the schoolbus. It's like a superstition. I know the whole thing sounds stupid but I'm afraid that if I stop, something bad will happen to me or my family.

What can I do? Am I going crazy or something?

Craig, aged 14

234 Willow Place
Bangor

Dear Craig

You are not the only one with this problem. It is called "obsessive compulsive disorder" (OCD). Most of us feel worried or superstitious at times, but with OCDs these feelings take over. You have compulsions—you have to repeat small acts over and over again to try and make uncomfortable thoughts go away. It's starting to interfere with your life, so I'm glad you wrote to me about it. Your feelings are not stupid at all. You are not alone, or going crazy, and you can get some help. There are websites and organisations that can give you more information and advice on OCDs. It may help to join a chatroom or self-help group, so you can talk to others who understand how you are feeling.

Sam, Agony Uncle

The Facts
Obsessive Compulsive Disorder (OCD)

✳ About three people in 100 have an OCD at some time: one in three problems start in childhood.

✳ Some doctors believe OCDs can happen when there is a shortage of the brain chemical serotonin: they may give serotonin-boosting drugs to help.

✳ Common compulsions include repeatedly washing hands, tidying, shutting doors, or checking locks.

✳ Check out the websites on page 29 for more information and help.

Your Views

Do you think Craig's problem is stupid? Do you think it's something that is easy to cover up, or will other people have noticed?

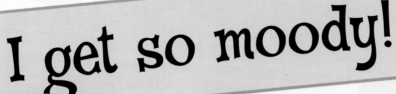

I get so moody!

Hi Kate. Just had another fight with mom.

Hi Josie. Oh no! What was it about?

Nothing really. She told me off for leaving lids off jars and I flipped!

Doesn't seem like much!

I know. Then I smashed some stuff up. Why am I like this?

Beats me. Glad I'm not your mom!

March 15 | **Josie's diary**

Another argument with Mom. Can't believe I got so angry with her over some jars! Then I smashed all the stuff on my dressing table—it was really stupid because they are my things and now I have to buy new ones! My period is due, and I think that makes things worse, because I feel it building up inside. I get sort of grouchy and snappy and I hate feeling that way.

The Facts

Moodiness

✳ We all get moody at times, and especially when our bodies are going through big changes, such as they do when we are growing up.

✳ Mood swings are a natural part of adolescence. They are caused by chemicals called hormones that are racing around in our bodies, preparing us to grow sexually. Changes in these chemicals (especially for girls around the time of their period) can lead to a buildup of tension and anger that is hard to control.

Top Tips

Preventing moodiness

⭐ Get a punching bag—it could just be a cushion: punch out your angry feelings!

⭐ Find some exercise you really enjoy. It could be rollerblading, basketball, or anything that gets you moving because exercise boosts feel-good hormones in our bodies.

⭐ Try breathing exercises to calm you: take slow, deep breaths.

⭐ Give your body a detox: avoid food and drinks that contain stimulants like caffeine or are high in additives. Try to eat a healthy diet with lots of fresh fruit and vegetables. Drink plenty of water—it flushes toxins through your body.

⭐ Listen to some calming music.

⭐ Keep a diary: it helps to write down how you are feeling.

⭐ Try some art therapy. Paint out your feelings in great sploshes of red or black, or whatever makes you feel better!

What makes you moody?

I get annoyed when my dad makes me do the dishes and I'm trying to watch something on TV. He never lets me do it later.
Sarah, aged 13

My best friend just drives me nuts sometimes. She's so bossy!
Tanya, aged 11

My teacher gives us too much homework. That makes me mad.
Sam, aged 14

Your Views

Do you ever feel moody? Do you know any good ways to keep calm?

21

I feel so afraid

197 Chalk Road
Lewiston

February 17

Trish's advice column
Sorted magazine
Cedar Bluffs

Dear Trish

A few months ago, my best friend Leanne nearly died in a car crash. When I found out about the accident I almost fainted and felt so sick. Leanne is getting better now but for a few weeks we thought she might die. I can't stop thinking about what could have happened to her. I don't sleep very well and when I do I have nightmares. I'm really scared that something else bad will happen. My dad has to drive a lot with his work and I worry that he will be in an accident. I hate going anywhere in the car. It's like I am getting scared to do normal things.

Kirsty, aged 12

Dear Kirsty,

When something frightening like this happens it is a terrible shock. You nearly lost your best friend, and you also lost your trust in things being okay. Going through the worry of Leanne being critically ill will have left you feeling very sensitive and emotional. These are natural feelings after a trauma like this. In time, you will rebuild your trust but it may help to talk to a counselor.

Trish, Agony Aunt

Top Tips

Coping with fear

★ Talk through your fears with a friend or someone you trust. Just talking about something can make it easier to cope.

★ It's natural to feel fear at times. It only becomes a problem if it stops us coping, or enjoying life.

★ Try writing down your fears in a diary or even painting them out in a picture that expresses how you feel.

★ Be kind to yourself: praise yourself when you overcome a fear, and forgive yourself when you don't!

What are you afraid of?

After my grandma died, I still wanted to go out with my friends, but I was afraid of leaving my mom in case something happened to her.

Carla, aged 13

I used to like horseback riding but I fell off my horse two years ago and I've never done it again. Sometimes I miss it.

Jen, aged 11

I got lost one day at the shopping mall. Now I'm afraid of getting lost. I know it's silly.

Ben, aged 9

Your Views

What's the best way to overcome your fears?

It's so embarrassing

Hi Gus. U ok? Were u embarrassed in class today?

Hi Harry. Nah, am fine. I was just hot.

U sure? Jackie and Ian thought u were blushing!

Nah. It's cool. C u tomorrow.

Gus's diary

April 15

I hate myself. I'm always blushing at the slightest thing, like if a girl starts talking to me, or when I put my hand up in class and everyone turns to look at me. Sometimes I don't even feel embarrassed but something happens and suddenly I can feel my face really burning. It's like someone with red-hot gloves on is pulling my skin tight. Even Harry has picked up on it now, and I don't want my friends making fun of me as well. I thought blushing was something only girls did, and it makes me feel like such a loser.

What happens when you get embarrassed?

> When I get embarrassed, I get really sweaty palms. It often happens at a party, meeting new people, or when I do a presentation in class.
>
> Jason, aged 12

> You just know when you are going to blush. You think, "Oh no, here I go!" It always seems to happen when you are trying to look cool.
>
> Gemma, aged 13

> I once nearly fainted on the hall stage in assembly. The whole school was looking at me. It was really embarrassing.
>
> Debra, aged 13

> When I get nervous, I start stuttering. It's worse when people try to finish your sentences for you.
>
> Imran, aged 13

Top Tips

Coping with embarrassment

★ Embarrassment and stress cause overheating—blushing happens as blood vessels get wider and blood rushes to the surface of the skin. The body may also sweat to cool itself down.

★ Help keep cool by wearing natural fabrics like cotton.

★ Avoid coffee, spicy foods, and alcohol.

★ The key is to relax: drop your shoulders, and concentrate on slowing down your breathing.

★ Blushing is very natural. If you do blush, don't get worked up about it—everyone does it sometimes. Try to laugh about it.

Your Views

What kind of things do you find embarrassing and why?

I get these panic attacks

From: Melanie17@w̶̶̶̶̶̶̶̶̶̶̶̶
To: kellym@w̶̶̶̶̶̶̶̶̶̶̶
Date: Monday, December 4
Subject: Sorry

Hi Kelly,

Sorry I didn't turn up on Saturday when you went shopping. It's just that I keep getting these panic attacks when I am out. They come on suddenly and my heart starts going fast and I feel like I can't breathe. It happened when I was shopping with Mom downtown and I thought I was going to faint. Now I am worrying that it might happen again. I am almost starting to feel like I don't want to go out anymore.

Anyway, please don't be annoyed with me and I hope to see you soon,

Melanie x

Hi Mel,

Don't worry, I'm not upset with you! It's hardly surprising you are getting these bad feelings with your brother being sick for so long. It must be hard going to see him in the hospital all the time and I guess your parents are really worried too. I read this magazine article about panic attacks, so I am attaching some info. Read a bit—it might help! If you feel like going shopping one Saturday, let me know. They've got some really cool stuff in that store we like!

Luv Kelly

The Facts
Panic attacks

✱ Panic attacks are your body's reaction to anxiety or stress.

✱ A panic attack can last anything from a few seconds up to 20 minutes.

✱ In a panic attack, the hormone adrenalin starts rushing around in the blood.

✱ Your heart rate and breathing get faster. You can go pale, have shaky legs, and feel hot, sweaty, and sick. You may need to rush to the bathroom.

Top Tips
Coping with a panic attack

★ Try to relax and go with the flow. If you tense up trying to resist it, the feelings will get worse.

★ Slow down your breathing—breathing into a paper bag can help.

★ Your doctor may be able to give you something to calm your anxiety, or recommend counseling.

Your Views

Why do you think Melanie has started having panic attacks?

Glossary

Adrenalin
A hormone that is released in the body in response to feelings of stress such as fear. It makes the heart and breathing rate speed up. It also causes an increase in sugar in the blood, which can be used by the body as fuel when more alertness or effort is needed.

Compulsions
When someone feels a strong need or desire to do something, which they cannot control.

Eating disorders
A range of problems and illnesses associated with eating and food.

Endorphins
Feel-good hormones that can be produced in the body by physical exercise.

Genetic
Related to genes, the part of our physical make-up that contains DNA and passes on characteristics from our parents.

Hormones
Chemicals made in the body that go around in our bloodstream.

Obsessive compulsive disorder (OCD)
An illness caused by stress or anxiety that causes obsessive thoughts and actions.

Periods
During puberty, a girl's uterus, or womb, develops a lining of blood and tissue in preparation for pregnancy. This lining is where a fertilized egg may implant itself after sexual intercourse. However, when there is no fertilized egg, the lining comes away each month and passes out through the vagina as a few spoonfuls of menstrual blood.

Puberty
The time when our bodies are changing, from the ages of around eight to 13 years old, preparing us to be capable of making babies.

Self-esteem
How we feel and think about ourselves.

Self-harm
Deliberately harming or injuring our bodies.

Serotonin
A brain chemical that affects mood.

Websites

www.familydoctor.org
Go to Parents & Kids and then click on Dealing with Feelings. Here you will find large number of articles about the home and family, thoughts and feelings, and emotions and behavior.

www.gmrdesign.com/ lifechallenges.org
A website that can be accessed any time, day or night, when you need support dealing with any life challenges, such as illness, relationship/family issues, dealing with death and grief, addiction, or abuse.

www.anxietypanic.com
This website is a resource that explains what anxiety and panic attacks are. Once you have read all of the information and understand your condition, you can decide on the best course of treatment for you.

www.rethink.org/
Information for young people on emotional problems, including exam stress, loneliness, and anger management.

http://psychcentral.com
Type "depression symptoms" into the search engine on this site. Information is available concerning teen health and self-esteem and why adolescents take risks. There is also information on trauma, eating disorders, sleep problems, stress, and anxiety and panic. Online support is also available from this site.

www.teenagehealthfreak.com
Lots of information on teenage problems, with answers and advice.

www.focusas.com/Hotlines.html
This site provides hotlines and helplines for a wide range of support organizations, such as Alcoholics Anonymous and Alateen Family Group, National Domestic Violence Hotline, and the National Hopeline Network, as well as many others.

Note to parents and teachers: Every effort has been made by the Publishers to ensure that these websites are suitable for children, that they are of the highest educational value, and that they contain no inappropriate or offensive material. However, because of the nature of the Internet, it is impossible to guarantee that the contents of these sites will not be altered. We strongly advise that Internet access is supervised by a responsible adult.

Index

This edition first published in 2008 by
Sea-to-Sea Publications
1980 Lookout Drive
North Mankato
Minnesota 56003

Copyright © Sea-to-Sea Publications 2008

Printed in China

All rights reserved.

Library of Congress Cataloging in Publication Data:

Powell, Jillian.
  Me and my feelings / by Jillian Powell.
    p.cm. -- (Problem page)
  Includes index.
  ISBN 978-1-59771-087-9
  1. Emotions--Juvenile literature. I. Title

BF561.P69 2007
152.4--dc22
                                    2006051286

9 8 7 6 5 4 3 2

Published by arrangement with the Watts Publishing Group Ltd, London.

Series editor: Sarah Peutrill
Art director: Jonathan Hair
Design: Rita Storey
Picture researcher: Diana Morris
Advisor: Wendy Anthony, Health education consultant

Picture credits: Caroline Birch/Life File Photos/Photographers Direct: 27. John Birdsall Photography: 11. Edward Bock/Corbis: 25. Paul Brown/Rex Features: 14. Antoinette Burton Photography/ Photographers Direct: 12. Ron Chapple/ Thinkstock/Alamy: 6t. Gary Doak/Topham: 13. Eastcott-Momatiuk/Image Works/ Topham: 8. Esbin-Anderson/Image Works/Topham: 23. Garo/Phanie/Rex Features: 22. David Hurrell/Rex Features: front cover b, 3, 16b. Image Works/Topham: 9. Steve Lyne/Rex Features: 15. Gabe Palmer/Corbis: 18. Phanie/Rex Features: 17. John Powell/Rex Features: 10. John Powell/Topham: 7, 20b. F. Sierakowski/Rex Features: 26. Mitch Wojanarowicz/Image Works/Topham: front cover t, 24.

Every attempt has been made to clear copyright. Should there be any inadvertent omission please apply to the publisher for rectification. All photos posed by models.